SIMULTANEOUS MOMENTS AND LIKE-MINDED SPIRITS

Sara van der Heide, March 2016
(Report on the censored seminar and library exhibition)

On December 13, 2015, on my invitation, a group of artists and the current directors of the Goethe-Institut Hong Kong and the Goethe-Institut Seoul gather in the seminar room of the Sun Yat-sen Library of Guangdong Province, China. We are here to discuss the presence of the German Library in Pyongyang, which was open between 2004 and 2009, but the underlying themes are peace and unification between North and South Korea. The day brings together several contributions and positions that both critically reflect on the presence of the German Library in Pyongyang, and propose a way of thinking aimed at transcending discourse that is prescribed by the lines of the nation-state, language, and geography. It will be a collective seminar realized through music, cooking, poetry, and conversations between guests who will meet each other for the first time here in China. But already a strong sense of connectivity between the participants is present.

During the day, Gabriele Stötzer speaks about her artistic activities and the role of women in the underground movement in the former GDR, and she describes her imprisonment after occupying a Stasi office. She speaks as a woman who offered some good years of her life for a larger cause, and as an important force behind the German unification movement. Stötzer's presentation is impressive. She was fighting against an inhumane, repressive system, which had nothing to do with the original ideology of communism, while still wanting to make beautiful things. She describes that for her there was no alternative other than what she did. As an audience, we feel pain and sadness, but most of all pride and deep respect while listening to her. In the days prior to the seminar, among the invited artists, we already discovered several

connections and similar life paths between us, but all situated in geographically different locations and under different regimes. Chankyong Park had also been imprisoned for his artistic activities under the South Korean regime. Robyn Haddon, a singer with an incredible voice from the United Kingdom, who is the youngest here, had a grandfather who served in the Korean War. Our moderator Hyunjin Kim, who is from South Korea, had a grandfather who was a communist and moved to North Korea. Recently, her family was approached to be part of a reunification program.

While it is clear for the rest of the world that North Koreans are living under a regime, it is less known how repressively the South Korean government operates. In a soft voice, Kyungman Kim describes how deeply the hate toward Communism and North Korea has penetrated South Korean society from a governmental level through the media and the education of young people. The formation of any kind of resistant labor movement has been rendered impossible, depriving South Koreans of any political form through which to organize themselves. Despite this, Kyungman Kim wishes to remain optimistic, but he knows that peace is very far away. A meeting like this, he explains, where peace and unification can be discussed, is difficult to organize in public space in South Korea. Also, unlike the German situation in 1989, when there were still many people who had relatives living on the other side of the Wall, in Korea there are very few people young enough to remember that they are missing parts of their families.

For myself, I am familiar with the feeling of being divided from my birth country and separated from family. After the Korean War, the United States and South Korea

"

set up a Christian adoption program for
abandoned children of American soldiers
and Korean mothers. Due to the influence
of Confucianism and because of past
colonization and occupation in Korea, there
is an emphasis on bloodlines in Korean
families. There is no place in South Korean
society for unwed or divorced mothers and
their children. Since the creation of the
adoption program, around 200,000 children
were put up for international adoption, a
practice continuing today, regardless of
the large economic growth in South Korea
and that children are being born to unwed
parents who are both Korean. I left South
Korea by airplane thirty-nine years ago.

Upstairs in the library itself, there are
several artistic contributions, reflecting
on and merging with the German Library.
With graphic designer Dongyoung Lee,
I have been working for some time on a
series of brochures to be presented in four
languages. Toward the opening we are
informed by the biennial organizers that
the brochures will not be printed and the
seminar will not be publically announced.
We are forced to accept these questionable
directives. The artists are here, and the
only other option is to cancel the entire
project and cause a scandal, which seems
the least interesting out of the two bad
options. I call a secret meeting with the
invited artists in a hotel room and we all
agree to continue with the seminar, which
eventually takes place under difficult
circumstances.

My last question was for Stefan Dryer,
the director of the Goethe-Institut Seoul is:
Could you describe the role of the Goethe-
Institut in Korea using the following analogy:
In a village there are two siblings fighting,
which one would you be?

A: the teacher
B: the mayor
C: the musician
D: the uncle

His answer is that he needs more time
to think about it.

ON CLOSING THE GAP

Anselm Franke, February 2016

From the late 1940s until 1989, the US-lead effort to contain communism and the subsequent anti-communist campaigns were the major force shaping and militarizing subjectivity globally. And in East Asia, the Cold War has not ended in 1989. This has become clear to me ever since I first visited the Korean Demilitarized Zone more than a decade ago, and even more so through recent collaborations and discussions with Chinese, Korean, and Japanese historians, artists, and intellectuals.

The subject of the formation of militarized subjectivities and the resistance against them has been explored in a series of works by Angela Melitopoulos in collaboration with Maurizio Lazzarato, which were first produced in the context of the exhibitions I curated such as *Animism* in 2011, and later for the Taipei Biennale and a recent exhibition in Gwangju, which is still on view until 2017. These works were not included in the 2014 Shanghai Biennale.

The ideological contours of the anti-communist campaign is well known, but in the West at least, there is little memory of the violence that was used to enforce this anti-communist agenda (aside, perhaps, from the Vietnam War—but is that war not remembered more for the effect it had on Western, rather than on Asian, societies?) Today, only the ideological struggle and the victory of liberal capitalism persists in collective memory in the West. On the other side, the shape of memory is rather different: the anti-communist wars and the military dictatorships that have been implanted in its wake have been well-remembered until recently, inscribed into a continuity of Western assaults since colonialism and nineteenth-century imperialism and a general conflict over modern identity under the spell of Orientalism. In a perverse reversal, it was opposition to this assault and its continuity on which Japan had built its claim for leadership in Asia, and its own imperial assault on its neighbors in the first half of the twentieth century. In the second half, the postwar realities of Asia, with Japan, South Korea, Taiwan, and several Southeast-Asian States having become client states of the US, the solidarity between China and North Korea was crafted on the grounds of this opposition. It was shaped in the binary terms of capitalism and communism, but beneath that confrontation was the older confrontation of Western colonialism that threw Asian civilizations into a deep and lasting crisis. China, in the course of events, has ever since been confronted with the challenge of building its ancient society anew, following the humiliating defeats suffered by the Qing dynasty in the Opium Wars in the 1840s, and its final breakdown in 1911. At this time, the truth-value of the entire order of the imperial past had to be radically questioned, and truth, as "common good," needed to be established on new foundations. The humiliation of colonial penetration in the nineteenth century still fuels Chinese politics today, even if in the eyes of the government the "great revival of the Chinese nation" that was inspiration for the last 200 years, seems now to be in reach.

Whatever one might think about North Korea—the very existence of this state is also a reminder of a history that dominant powers and subject-formations might rather want to obscure and forget (or leave as fuel to nationalist parties ready to be instrumentalized, or perhaps as templates for myths and identities that are allowed to make their second or third historical appearance as a spectacle or tourist attraction). And today, it appears that China is one of these dominant powers that sooner or later might prefer to dissociate their own official historical memory from that of North Korea and its path of antagonism—or at least define that legacy on their own terms. This is why the division of Korea is an open wound in which history lives on as a battle of imperial schemes and the tragedies of resistance.

It is perhaps impossible to say exactly what is going on in China ideologically and what defines its shifting relationship with both the West and North Korea. It is impossible because the country does not speak or think with one voice, even the Party does not. Yet it is clear is that the country has chosen a different path since 1978, and that it does not want to tie its fate to a nuclear North Korea. While there is no place here to discuss the diplomatic relationship between the two countries and the details of their ties and disagreements, it is clear that China has left the path of opposition and antagonistic resistance to Western and US hegemony, at least on the surface, and has chosen instead the path of market assimilation and mimetic adaption to world capitalism as a strategy to revival and power, with considerable success.

So where is China heading? Towards a truly novel mixture of technologically enhanced management and authoritarian government, fuelled by nationalist mythologies and traditions. China is following Singapore on the path of using Total Information Awareness technology and strategy beyond
① military aims, geared towards the creation of a cybernetically managed and surveilled "harmonious society." It may well claim that as an alternative form of democracy; this technology combines Mao's "mass line," recently revived by President Xi Jinping, with the ever-deeper market integration, as also pursued by the US and EU. In 2020, China aims to activate its Sesame score program,
② a social credit-rating system run by Alibaba, still in its test phase, that eventually will

expand to all areas of life, aimed at nothing less than instigating virtuous behavior in the Chinese subject. The aim here is to measure and economize "trust" (similar plans exist in Switzerland—where else?), and the president also declared that this "trust" shall act as a moral glue binding together the future Chinese society. President Xi Jinping here puts his predecessors talk of "scientific development" and the "harmonious society" (*hexie shehui*), which were widely supported and yet perceived as "weak," on pragmatic feet. Ideologically, he moves increasingly further away from Marxism with "Chinese characteristics," while at the same time re-affirming Mao's legacy. Yet this salvaging of Mao's legacy, somewhat paradoxically, goes hand in hand with the revival of traditional Chinese culture and Confucianism—the very legacy that was, for more than a century, regarded as the key obstacle in Chinese modernisation, and blamed for its inferiority in the confrontation with the West.

When Xi speaks of the glue that will bind Chinese society together, his language echoes a long history of ideology and techniques of social engineering. In ancient Chinese history, the literati-bureaucrats, under the protection of the emperor and often in conflict with local aristocracy, were those who first turned the vast amount of peasants primarily attached to the bonds of kinship into a society. They did this primarily by conceiving large-scale engineering projects such as river dredging—indeed the Chinese nation was first crafted in ancient times in response to the floods of the Yellow River. These were conceived as measures to "control the ten thousand things" and "put in order heaven and earth." This order is reflected in the macro- and microcosmos, starting with the self and reaching all the way through society's institutions to the environment. Modernity derailed this always-precarious order of heaven and earth. If a key concern of the Confucian tradition had been the attempt to find a remedy for the persistent failure to "close the circle" and realize in social order the "oneness" of their cosmic vision, then this circle, and indeed any social bond, has been called into question in modernity. With the revival of Confucian "values" to official state doctrine that we are witnessing now, the time of this questioning, and hence of a certain modernity, appears to be over.

Today the ancient Confucian vision seems to be within reach—but in the form of a mega-machine that is as "ecological" as it is Orwellian. And whether the Chinese population will go along with this new vision is indeed highly questionable. But what might be its resources for resistance? We are currently witnessing the intensification of yet another genealogy: namely, that ever since the ancient literati-bureaucrats, and long before the Western nations existed, China has produced an enormous quantity of documents, data, and statistical analysis about its population. Today's Sesame Credit is a continuation of this legacy in social engineering and the building of a state-machine, like the China Brain Project, too: a massive undertaking in the quest of leadership in artificial intelligence for which China's Baidu is teaming up with the government and the military. Billions of people, especially in China, use their cellphones as socio-metric sensors, and using this data it is possible to make crucial advances in the understanding of human-machine interaction, big data analysis, automated driving, smart medical diagnosis, smart drones, and robotics technologies for ③ both military and civilian use, and so forth. It is the authoritarian framework that gives Baidu's quest for AI a crucial advantage over its competitors like Google.

For the Confucian scholar, it was clear that there was a fundamental oneness in the order of the cosmos, and that this oneness ought to be reflected and realized in the social order. But they struggled acutely in realizing this vision of harmony, in closing the circle against the backdrop of the actually existing plurality—cognitively, like rough waters on the open sea, and socially, a persistence of "moral wilderness"; this is the rhetoric used by Xi today, which contrasts rather starkly with the rhetorics of Kim Jong Un. The awareness of this gap between their ideals of social order, and this wilderness within and without, crucially informed the ritual and routine of bureaucratic administration and attitude. The question today, I believe, is not so much the critique of "universal" values, but whether there is a future for that gap: because it is only in the awareness of this gap that the endangered dream of democracy can nest.

[1] Shane Harris, "The Social Laboratory," *Foreign Policy*, July 29, 2014, http://www.foreignpolicy.com/2014/07/29/the-social-laboratory.

[2] Darlene Storm, "ACLU: Orwellian Citizen Score, China's Credit Score System is a Warning for Americans," *Computer World* October 7, 2015, http://www.computerworld.com/article/2990203/security/aclu-orwellian-citizen-score-chinas-credit-score-system-is-a-warning-for-americans.html.

[3] Bien Perez, "'China Brain' Project Seeks Military Funding as Baidu Makes Artificial Intelligence Plans" *South China Morning Post*, April 16, 2015, http://www.scmp.com/lifestyle/technology/article/1728422/head-chinas-google-wants-country-take-lead-developing.

CHINA AND MUCH MORE

Gabriele Stötzer, February 2016
(English translation, followed by the original German text)

I am in awe the whole time. I am in China. "Behind the Wall," as I am humming Wolf Biermann's lyrics to myself, against whose expatriation from the GDR I had protested in 1976 and for which I spent a year in prison. That's how China began, with the wall, which separated East and West Germany back then and which fell in 1989.

An art project by the South Korean/Dutch artist Sara van der Heide for the 1st Asia Biennial/5th Guangzhou Triennial brought me to Guangzhou. Sara van der Heide had conveyed the Goethe-Institut Pyongyang's German Library, which had been established in North Korea in 2004, to the public library in the old part of town and she had invited artists, among others from South and North Korea and the formerly divided Germany, for artistic contributions. Mine was to report about our female artist group in Erfurt at the end of the '80s under the GDR dictatorship, a state that provided socialist realism as the art form for worshipping socialism as ideology. If one wanted to produce or live something of one's own, one had to go underground, which meant to perform in private apartments or church premises. We developed art forms like performances or fashion-object-shows, which could be set up quickly and taken with again. We were mobile until the occupation of the first Stasi headquarters on December 4, 1989, which was initiated by five women from Erfurt. I thought that China would be an appropriate place to speak about our experiences. Flight paid, accommodation in one of the best hotels in the city center—what more could I have wanted.

But when I arrived on site, the artist Sara van der Heide called us into a hotel room and told us that our participation had been cancelled from the public program of the biennial. She would not be allowed to distribute her German, English, Korean, and Chinese brochures. We could nevertheless hold the seminar, if all artists present would decide upon it collectively, but without publicity and with only a small number of invited Chinese guests. Mainly just for us, the Chinese accompanying team, and the other artists of the exhibition. We were struck. The Wall in Germany had fallen twenty-five years ago, however that past emotion was back right away: the prohibitions, the allegations of being something dangerous. Then the Dutch artist Louwrien Weijers opened with: "To make no demands but to perform." And I felt a certainty, which had grown out of many fights and efforts of my own, which regardless of state and religion constitutes all artists; to go public and to not resign.

The biennial, in which Sara van der Heide's library project was included, was opened by a young Chinese woman in a traditional, elegant Chinese dress, but in fact the important politicians and art and cultural organizers were standing in the front row and were all men. This I also knew from before. Earlier on we had talked in our group about feminism. Louwrien Wijers reckoned that she was not a feminist but that every woman is strong by herself. I said, "In your generation it was like that: without female role models, lone female warriors. That is possible in a democracy but in a dictatorship one only survives in a group." Apart from that I preferred the term feminist, with which I had been labelled next to sexist and psychopath as an artist from the underground scene, as the most pleasant. In my talk I told at first about the elementary power of women, who I had met in prison. All passions and possibilities for good and evil—these attributes that

under socialism we only ever attributed
to our capitalist enemies behind the Wall
are part of us, close to our own lineage.
We need to take responsibility, therefore,
otherwise fear of the other and the others,
and confusion before the moment of real
danger will rule us. A Korean performer said
in Guangzhou, "If we allow freedom of
speech, then capitalism arrives." We would
have had a lot to discuss but we departed
a day after the performance, glad to be
able to escape these pompous, self-centered
politics.

But China touched me deeply on another
level: through the encounter and experience
with individuals, whether Chinese or foreign.
The consistency of the self, the encounter
with these circumstances, and the respect
for each other were an important experience
for me.

CHINA UND NOCH VIEL MEHR

Ich staune die ganze Zeit. Ich bin in China.
„Hinter der Mauer," wie ich den Liedtext
von Wolf Biermann vor mir her summe,
gegen dessen Ausbürgerung aus der DDR
ich 1976 protestierte und dafür ein Jahr
im Gefängnis war. So fing China an, mit
der Mauer, die Ost- und Westdeutschland
damals trennte und 1989 fiel.

Ein Kunstprojekt der südkoreanisch/
holländischen Künstlerin Sara van der Heide
für die erste Asia Biennale und die fünfte
Guangzhou Triennale hatten mich nach
Guangzhou geführt. In der chinesischen
Stadtbibliothek im alten Teil der Stadt
hatte Sara van der Heide die deutsche
Bibliothek des Goethe-Instituts Pjöngjang,
die in Nordkorea 2004 eingerichtet wurde,
nach Guangzhou transportiert und Künstler
u.a. aus Süd- und Nordkorea und des
einst geteilten Deutschlands für artistic
contributions eingeladen. Mein Beitrag war

von unserer Künstlerinnengruppe Erfurt
Ende der 80er Jahre in der Zeit der DDR-
Diktatur zu berichten. Ein Staat, der den
sozialistischen Realismus als Kunstform
vorgab mit dem der Sozialismus als
Ideologie verherrlicht wurde. Wenn man
etwas Eigenes produzieren und leben
wollte, musste man in den Untergrund
gehen, das hieß in privaten Wohnungen oder
in Gebäuden der Kirche aufzutreten. Wir
entwickelten Kunstformen wie Performances
oder Modeobjektshows, die man schnell
entstehen lassen und wieder mitnehmen
konnte. Wir waren mobil bis zur Besetzung
der ersten Stasizentrale am 4.12.1989 in
der DDR, die 5 Erfurter Frauen initiierten.
Ich hatte durchaus die Idee, dass ich in
China am rechten Ort wäre, um von unseren
Erfahrungen zu sprechen. Flug bezahlt,
Unterbringung in einem der besten Hotels im
Zentrum der Stadt—was wollte ich mehr.

Aber als ich dort ankam, rief uns die
Künstlerin Sara van der Heide in ein
Hotelzimmer und sagte, dass wir aus
dem öffentlichen Programm der Biennale
gestrichen waren. Sie dürfe ihre deutsch-,
englischen-, koreanischen- und chinesischen
Broschüren nicht austeilen. Trotzdem könnten
wir das Seminar durchführen, wenn die
anwesenden Künstler sich kollektiv dafür
entscheiden würden, jedoch ohne Werbung
und nur mit einigen wenigen eingeladenen
chinesischen Gästen. Im Wesentlichen
für uns, das chinesische Begleitteam und
die anderen Künstler der Ausstellung. Wir
waren betroffen. Die Mauer in Deutschland
ist nun 25 Jahre gefallen, trotzdem war
das Gefühl von damals sofort wieder da,
die Verbote, die Unterstellungen etwas
Gefährliches zu sein. Dann begann die
holländische Künstlerin Louwrien Weijers mit:
„Keine Forderungen stellen und auftreten."
Und ich spürte ein aus vielen eigenen
Kämpfen und Überwindungen gewachsenes
Selbstverständnis, das unabhängig von Staat
und Religion alle Künstler ausmacht. In die
Öffentlichkeit gehen und nicht aufgeben.

Die Biennale, an welcher Sara van der
Heides Bibliotheksprojekt teil hat, wurde von

einer jungen Chinesin in einem traditionellen
eleganten chinesischen Kleid eröffnet, aber
die eigentlichen wichtigen Politiker und
Kunstorganisatoren standen in der ersten
Reihe und waren nur Männer. Das kannte
ich auch von früher. Vorher hatten wir in
unserer Gruppe über Feminismus geredet.
Louwrien Wijers meinte, dass sie keine
Feministin wäre, sondern jede Frau alleine
für sich stark ist. Ich sagte: „In eurer
Generation war das so, ohne weibliche
Vorbilder, Einzelkämpferinnen. Das ist in
einer Demokratie möglich, aber in einer
Diktatur überlebt man nur in einer Gruppe."
Außerdem war mir der Begriff Feministin,
neben Sexistin oder Psychopathin, mit denen
man mich als Künstlerin der Untergrundszene
betitelte, der angenehmste.

In dem Vortrag erzählte ich erst von der
elementaren Kraft von Frauen, die ich
im Gefängnis kennengelernt hatte. Alle
Leidenschaften und Möglichkeiten zum Guten
und Bösen, das in dem sinnenfeindlichen
Sozialismus immer nur die anderen besaßen
und damals hinter der Mauer beim
kapitalistischen Klassenfeind saß, sind in
uns, hautnah, bis ins eigene Geschlecht.
Wir müssen selber dafür Verantwortung
übernehmen, sonst regiert uns die Angst vor
den und dem anderen und eine Verwirrung
vor dem Moment der wirklichen Gefahr.
Ein koreanischer Performer sagte in
Guangzhou: „Wenn wir die Meinungsfreiheit
zulassen, dann kommt der Kapitalismus." Wir
hätten noch viel diskutieren können aber
reisten nach dem Auftritt am anderen Tag
zurück, froh dieser pompösen, sich selbst
bespiegelnden Politik entrinnen zu können.

Aber China hat mich auf eine andere Art
tief berührt. Durch die Begegnung und
Erfahrung mit einzelnen Menschen.
Chinesisch oder anders ausländisch—die
Unbeirrbarkeit des Selbst, die Beugung vor
den nun mal angetroffenen Umständen und
die Achtung füreinander waren ein wichtiges
Erlebnis für mich.

FILMMAKER KYUNGMAN KIM
IN RESPONSE TO THE REQUEST TO TAKE PART IN
THE GERMAN LIBRARY PYONGYANG IN GUANGZHOU

From: Kyungman Kim
Subject: Re: message for Kyungman Kim
Date: 4 Oct 2015 21:31
To: Sara van der Heide

Dear Sara,

Thank you for your reply and links to
your project.
I'd like to answer your question.
I was an elementary school student
when the Chun Doohwan regime had begun.
At that time, most older-generation
people hated the red color itself.
Even the red color was not banned by law,
but it was not natural to wear red clothes
or to use red color too much in painting.
Old people were released from the phobia of
red in 2002 because the World Cup was held
in Korea, and there was a huge cheering
party who were wearing red shirts.
The old generation may have recognized
the cheering party as a patriotic group.
Ironically, the motto of the cheering party
was, "Be the Reds!"
I guess the reason for this was from
the Korean War and socialization about it.
So many innocent people were killed
brutally because they had been regarded
as communists.
And so much hatred toward North Korea
was in the air for many decades, as you
have seen in my film, and even now
it is still continuing.
When I was a student in the public
education system for twelve years, I had to
learn about how evil North Korea was.
The name of the class was ironically
"the Moral" or "National Ethics."
When I was a high-school student,
I had to learn bayonet skills.
It was a regular curriculum for every boy in
high school.
After that I had to enter the military service.
These are very common experiences of
my generation.
And nowadays, the relationship between
the two Koreas is worse then it has ever
been, since 1991.
For many years, on the fifteenth of every
month there has been an air-raid siren for
evacuation drill.
But we just ignore this and continue our
daily life even though there is still the
possibility of a war.
It is not a good condition for happiness.
Many people are suffering due to
unemployment or discharge.
The labor law has been useless in Korea
because even the government doesn't obey.
Because of the anti-communism, labor
movements and social movements have been
blocked effectively.
Many people have been killed, jailed,
or fined.
You can imagine what else is forbidden when
even the color red itself is a problem.
And you could imagine wondering how could
the mind and the thoughts of an individual
be free under this system?
I like your ideas about the project.
And I wish my film can be useful for your
exhibition.
I will wait for further news from you.

Warm wishes,
Kyungman

DOCUMENTATION OF THE GERMAN LIBRARY PYONGYANG & THE SEMINAR   독일평양문화원

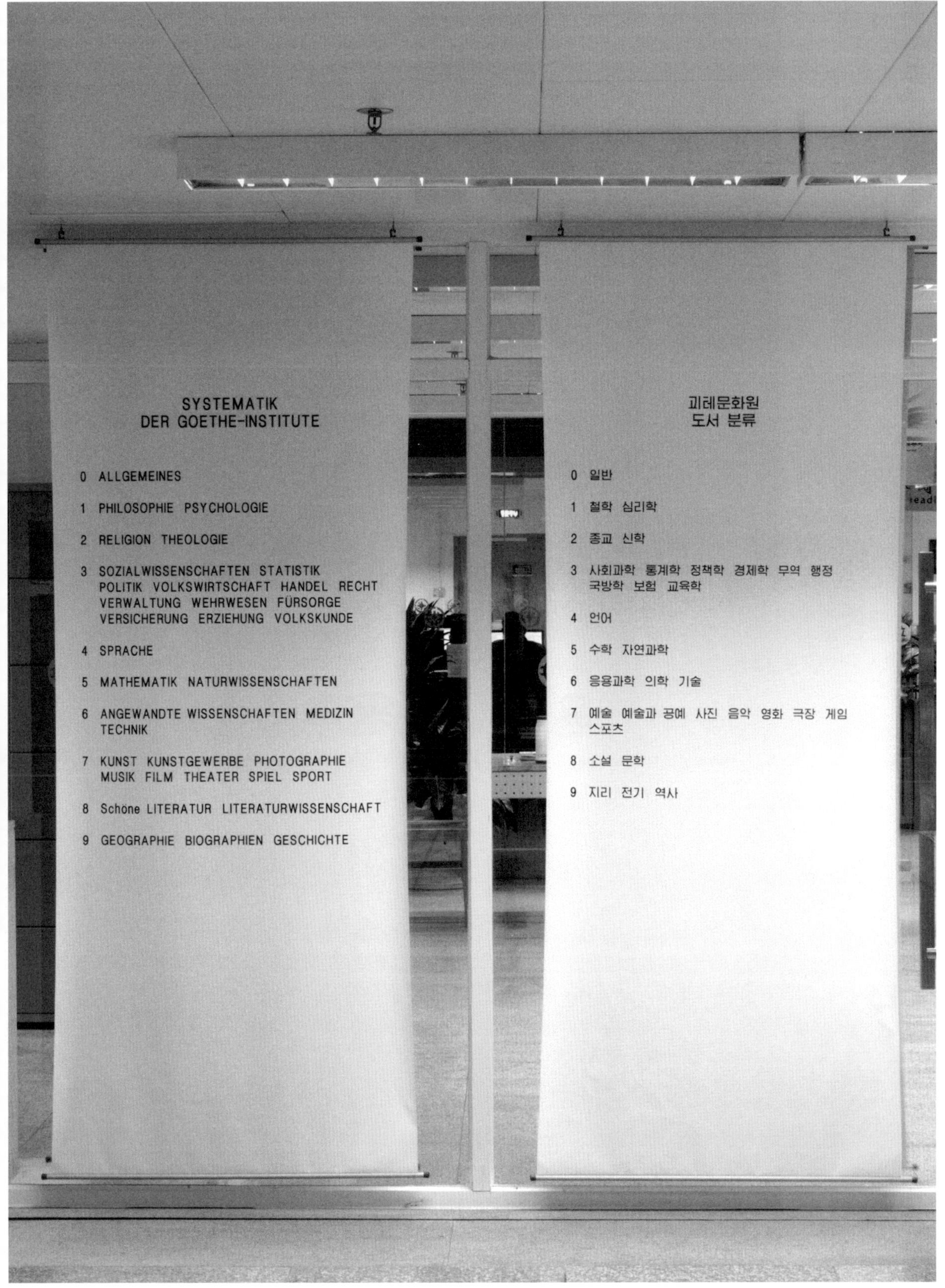

Sara van der Heide (i.c.w. Dongyoung Lee), *The German Library Pyongyang*, 2015,
imaginary transformation of the location: all institutional printed matter written in Chinese is replaced by Korean.

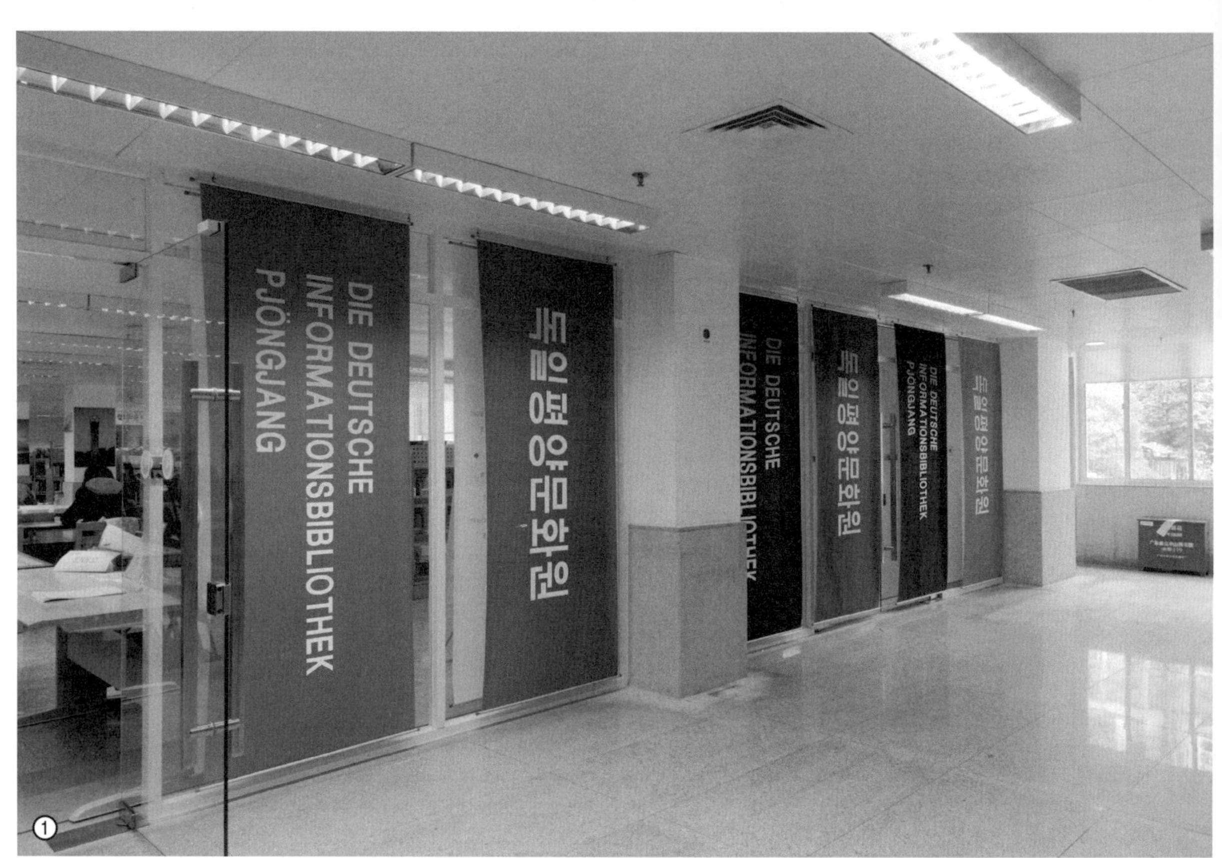

1–5   Sara van der Heide (i.c.w. Dongyoung Lee), *The German Library Pyongyang*,
       2015, imaginary transformation of the location: all institutional printed matter written in
       Chinese is replaced by Korean.
6,7   Sara van der Heide (i.c.w. Dongyoung Lee), *The German Library Pyongyang Database*,
       2015, reprint of the original database of the library in Pyongyang, 5.000 cards and
       index catalogs.
8   Publication: *Conversation Pieces between Erich Honecker and Kim Il Sung*, 2015,
       published by Back to the Mountain Publishing House.

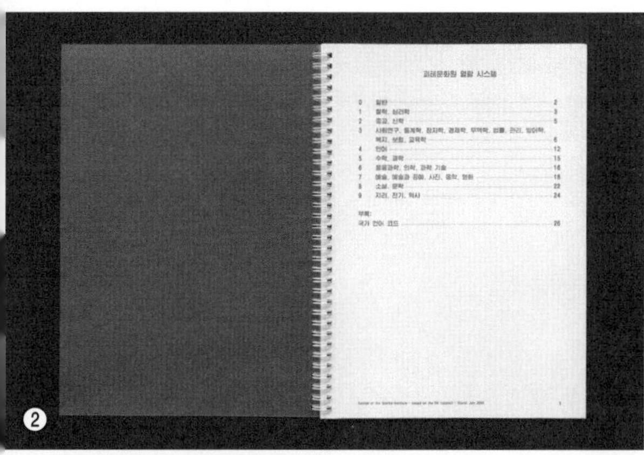
괴테문화원 활용 시스템

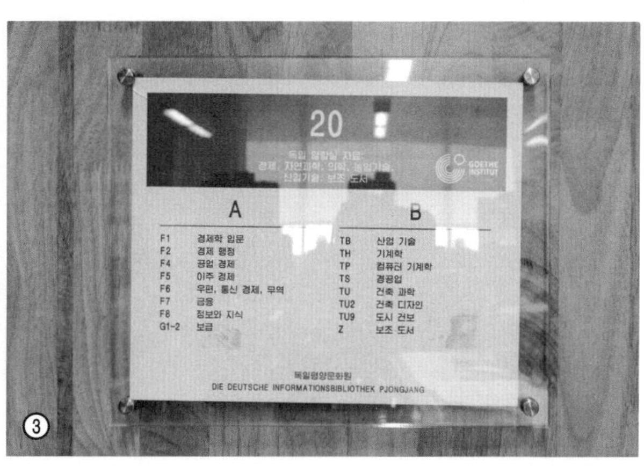
20
A
B
F1   경제학 입문
F2   경제 행정
F4   공업 경제
F5   이주 경제
F6   우편, 통신 경제, 무역
F7   금융
F8   정보와 지식
G1-2 보급
TB   산업 기술
TH   기계학
TP   컴퓨터 기계학
TS   경공업
TU   건축 과학
TU2 건축 디자인
TU9 도시 건보
Z   보조 도서
독일평양문화원
DIE DEUTSCHE INFORMATIONSBIBLIOTHEK PJONGJANG

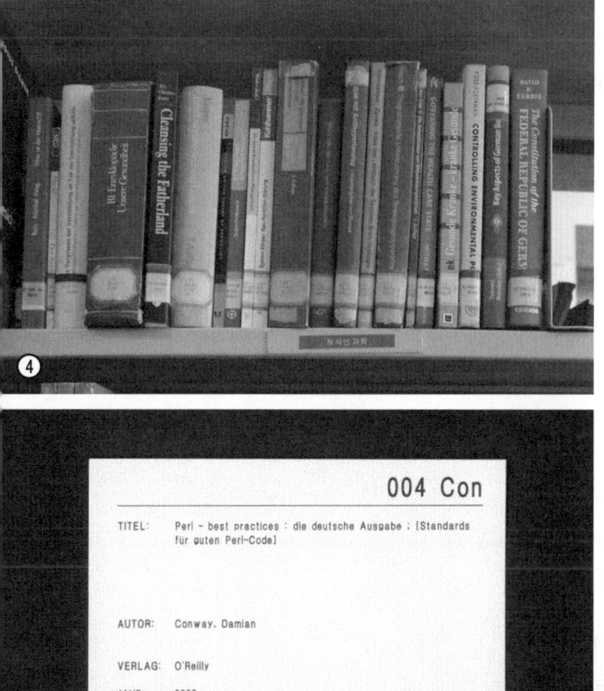

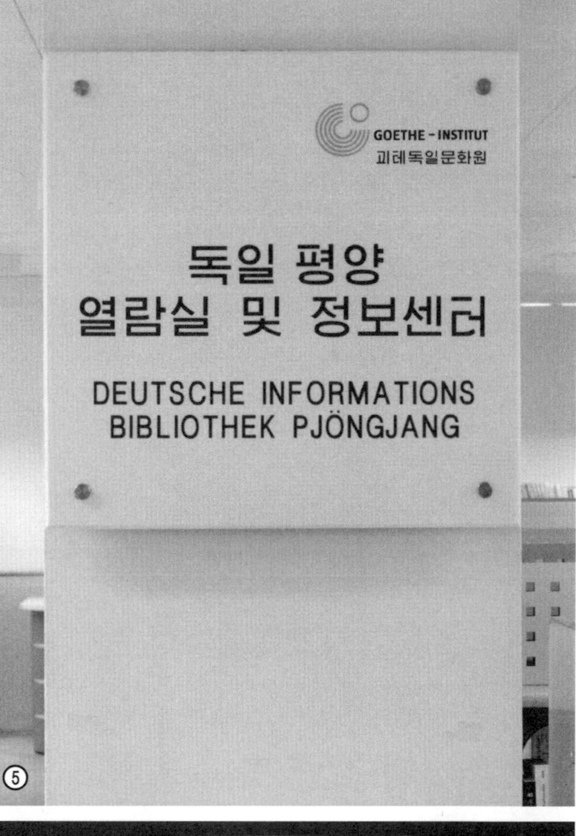
GOETHE – INSTITUT
괴테독일문화원
독일 평양
열람실 및 정보센터
DEUTSCHE INFORMATIONS
BIBLIOTHEK PJÖNGJANG

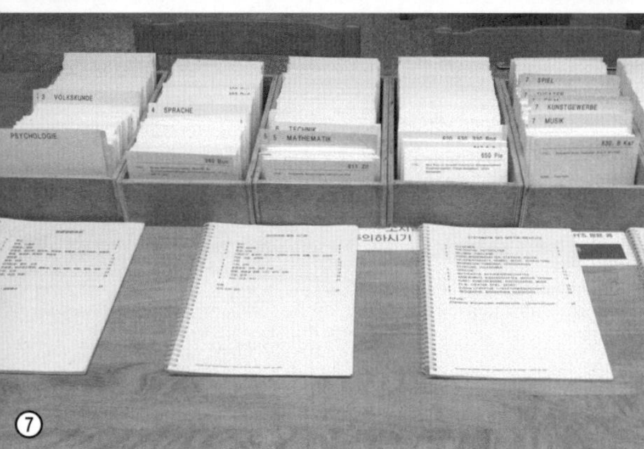
004 Con
TITEL: Perl – best practices : die deutsche Ausgabe ; [Standards
         für guten Perl-Code]
AUTOR: Conway, Damian
VERLAG: O'Reilly
JAHR: 2006
ISBN: 3-89721-454-7

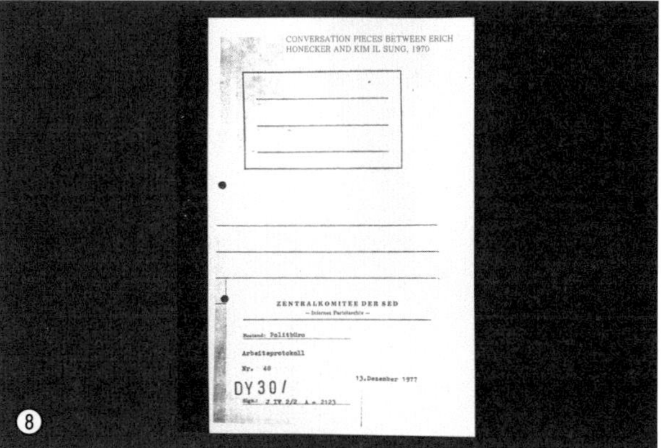
CONVERSATION PIECES BETWEEN ERICH
HONECKER AND KIM IL SUNG, 1970

ZENTRALKOMITEE DER SED
– Internes Parteiarchiv –

Bestand: Politbüro
Arbeitsprotokoll
Nr. 40   13.Dezember 1977
DY 30/
Sgn.: J IV 2/2 A a 2123

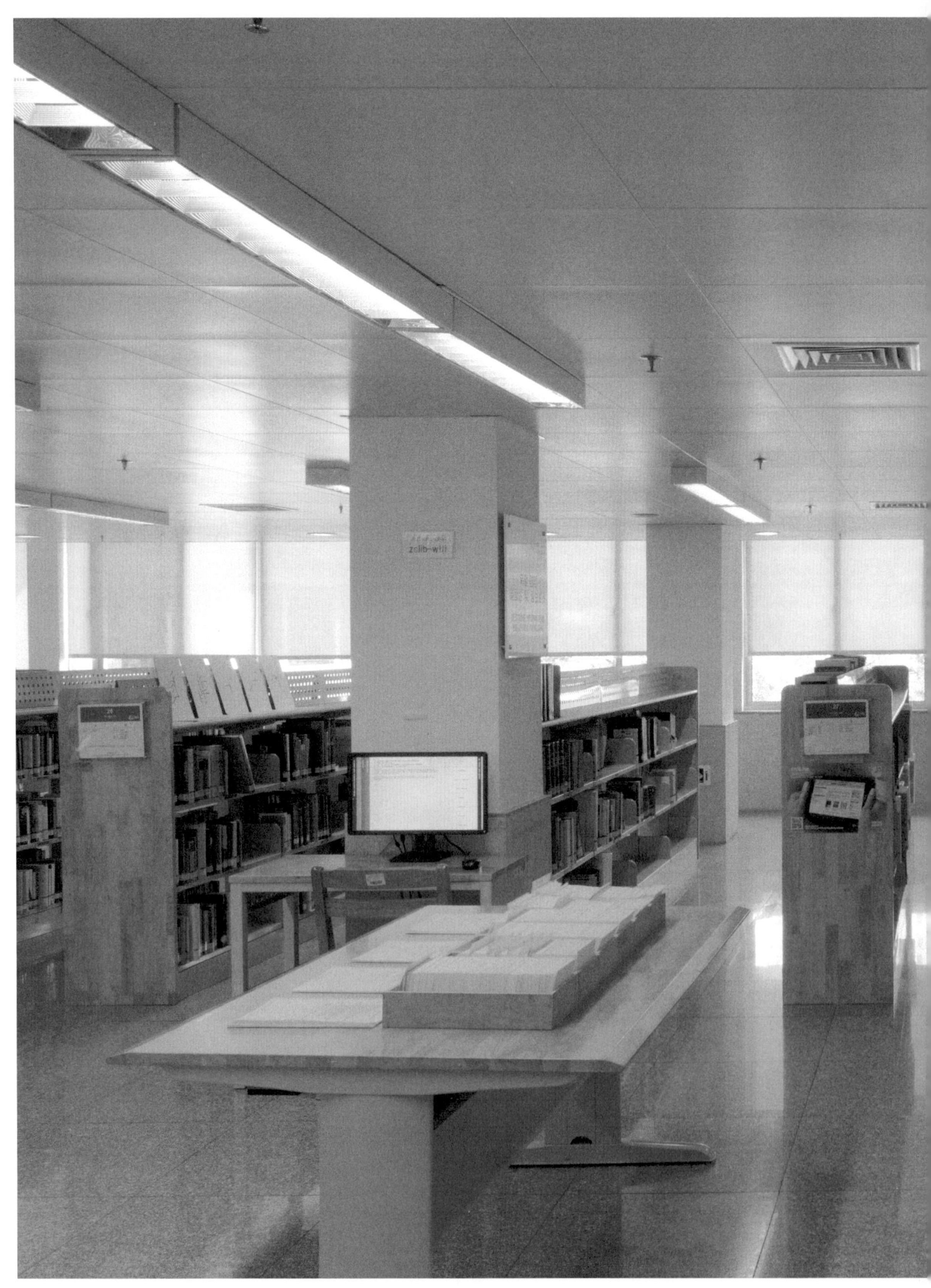

Sara van der Heide, installation of *The German Library Pyongyang*, with digital database, produced in collaboration with Kristian Johansen and Dongyoung Lee.

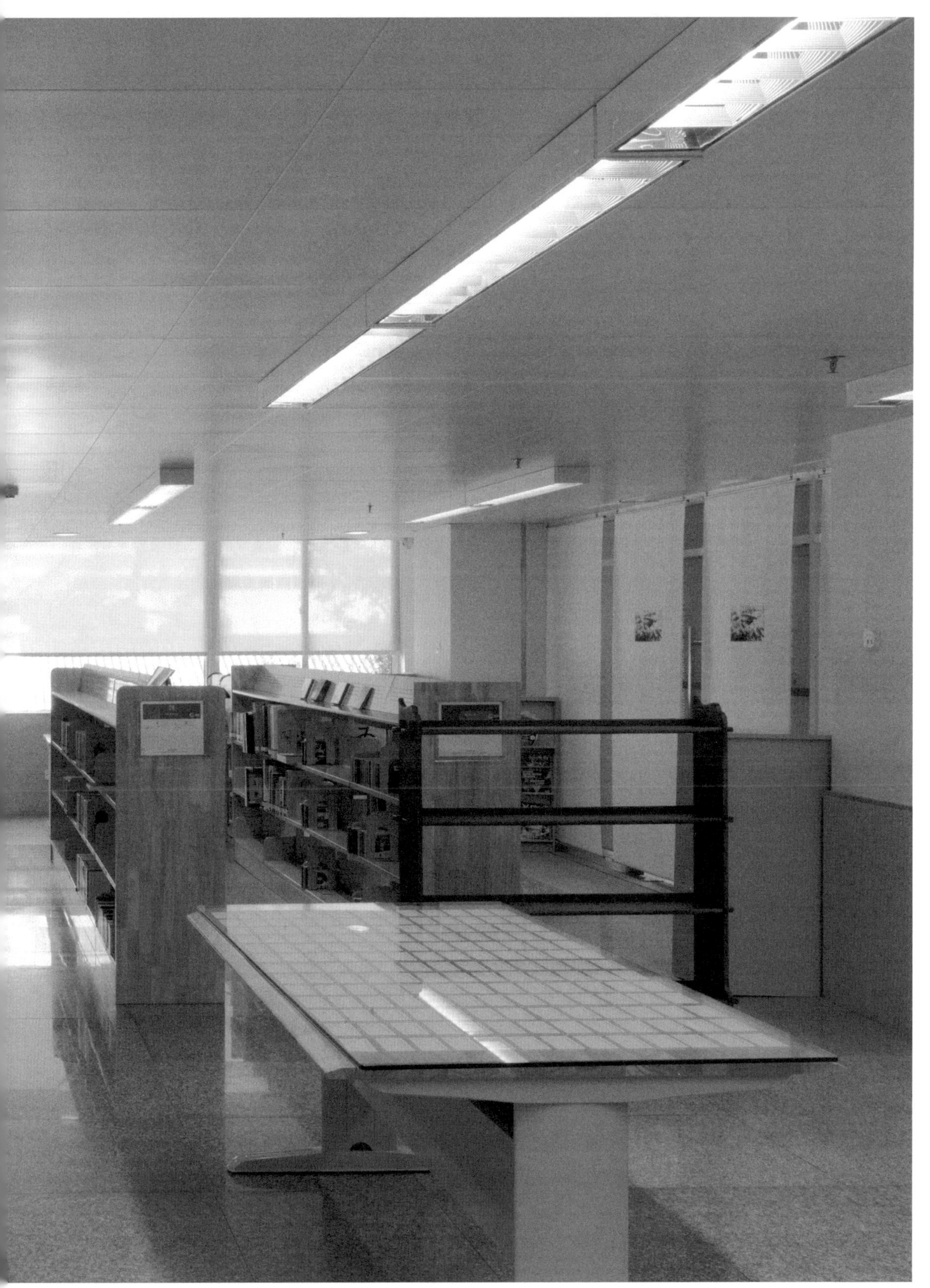

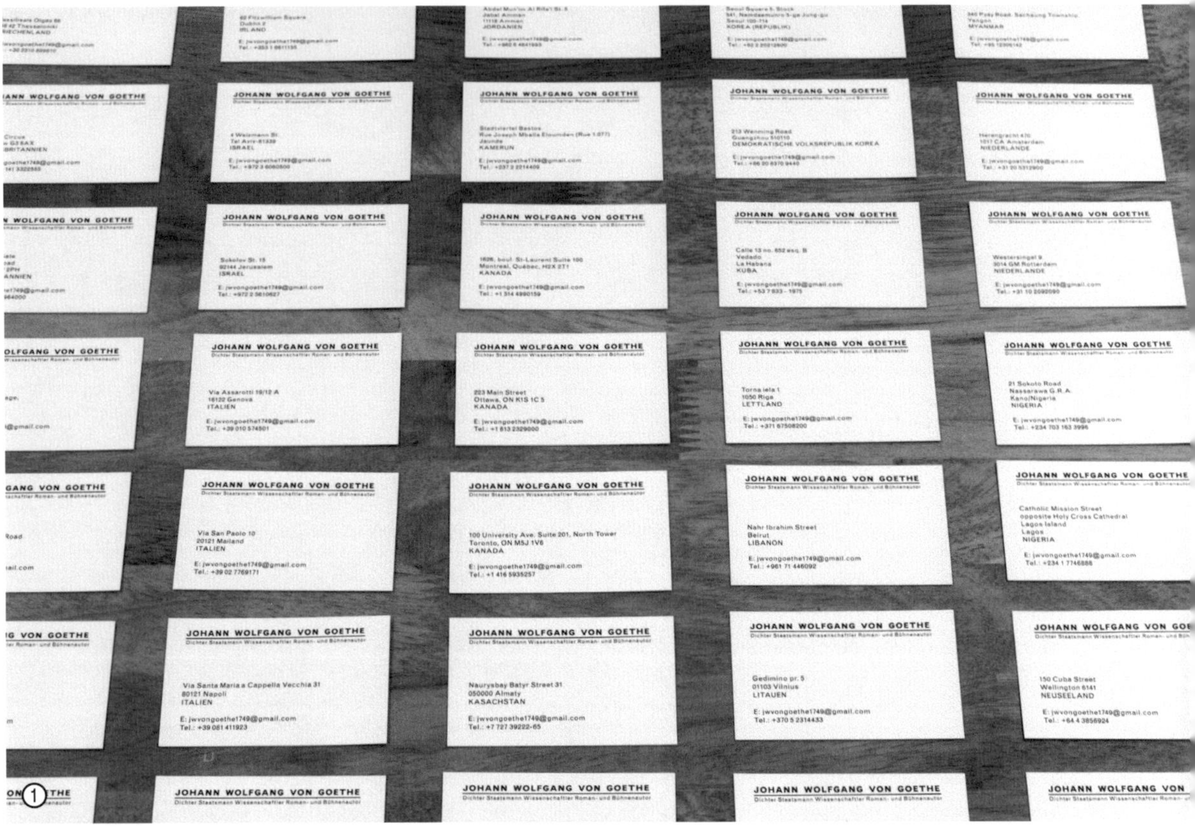

JOHANN WOLFGANG VON GOETHE
Dichter Staatsmann Wissenschaftler Roman- und Bühnenautor

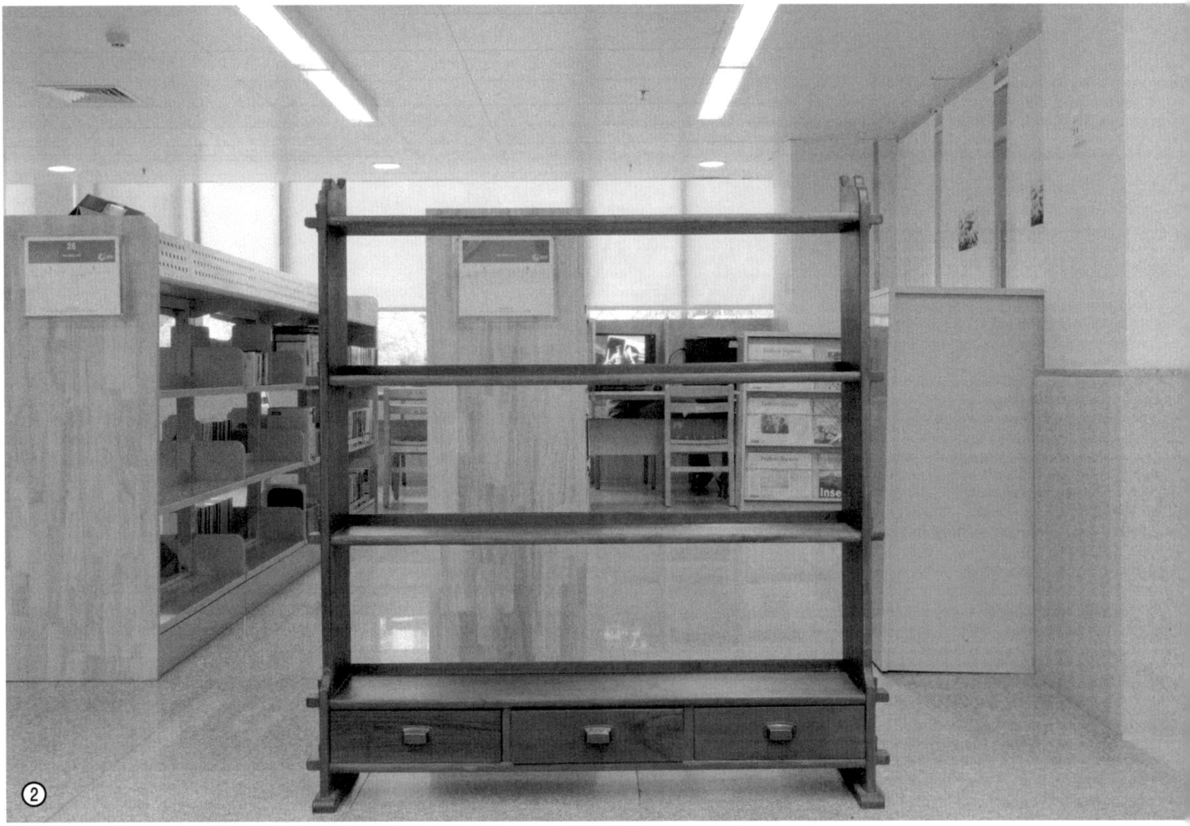

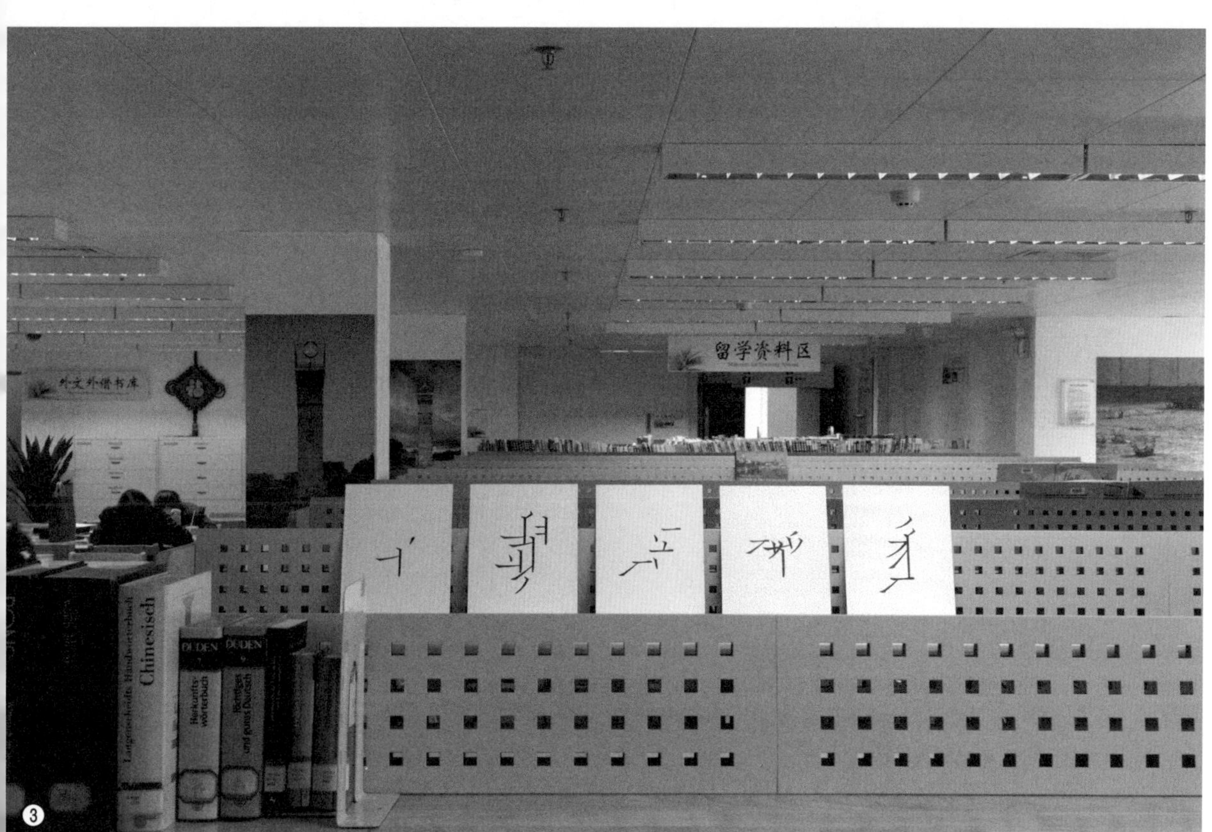

1   Sara van der Heide, *Johann Wolfgang von Goethe Has a House in 169 Places*, 2015,
     169 business cards, displayed in alphabetical order.
2   Chen Tong, *The True Bookcase*, 2015, bookcase and video.
3   Sora Kim, *Abstract Reading*, 2015, printed text.

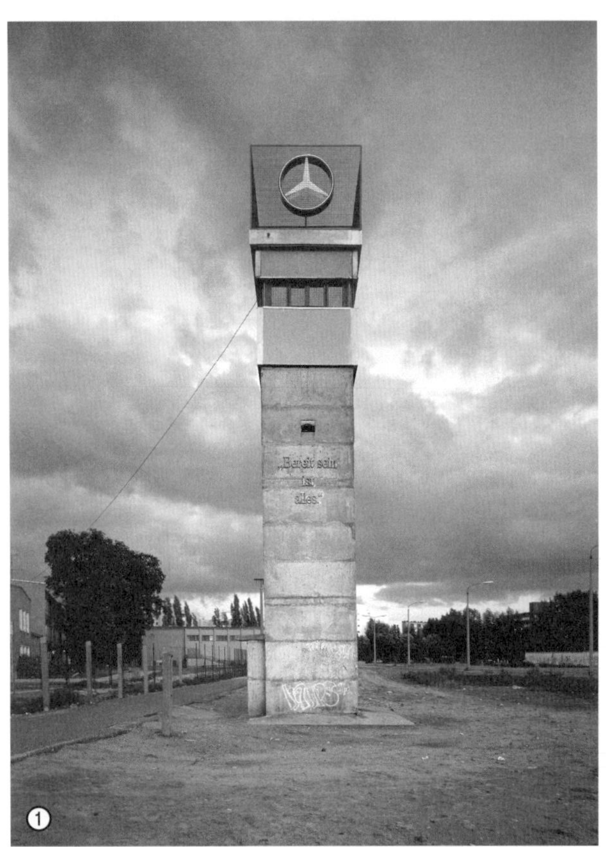
„Kunst ist
alles."

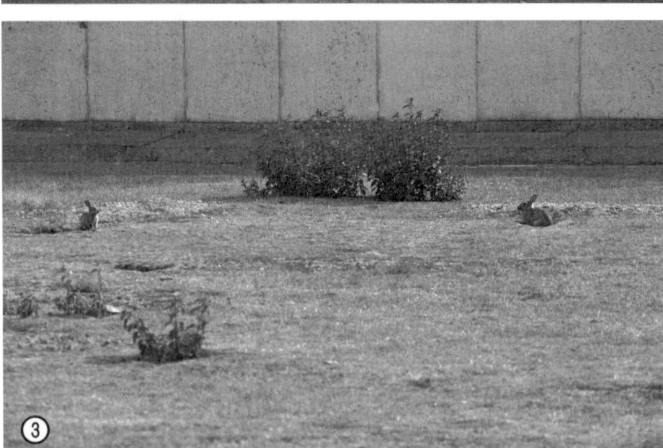
„Kunst
bleibt
Kunst."

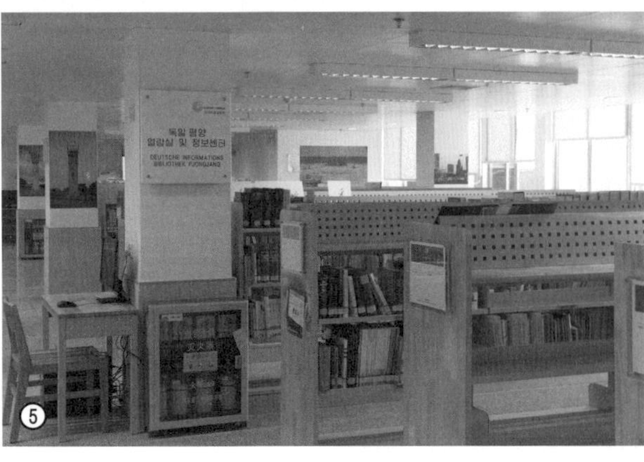

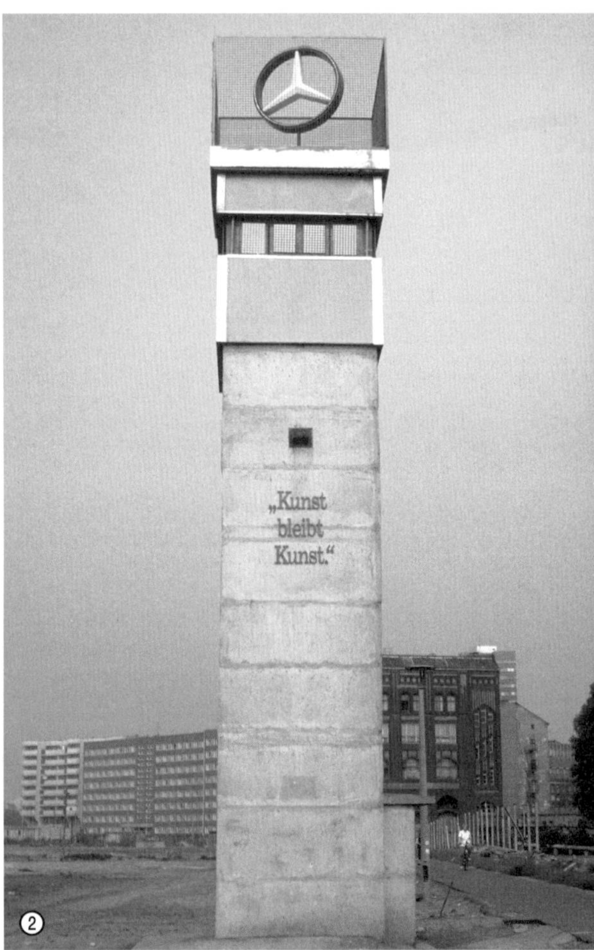
SFB

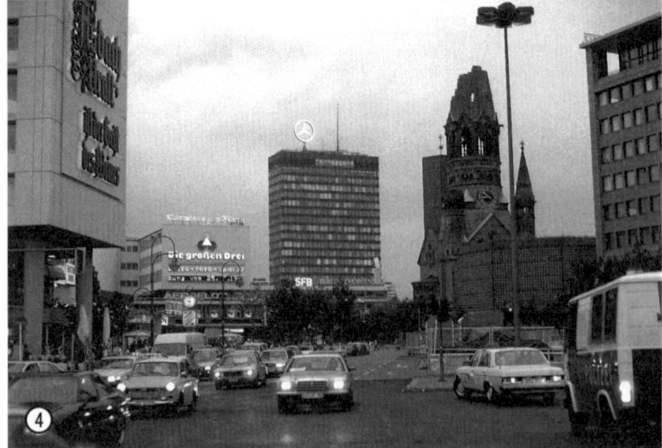
독일 문화
열람실 및 정보센터
DEUTSCHE INFORMATIONS
BIBLIOTHEK PJONGJANG

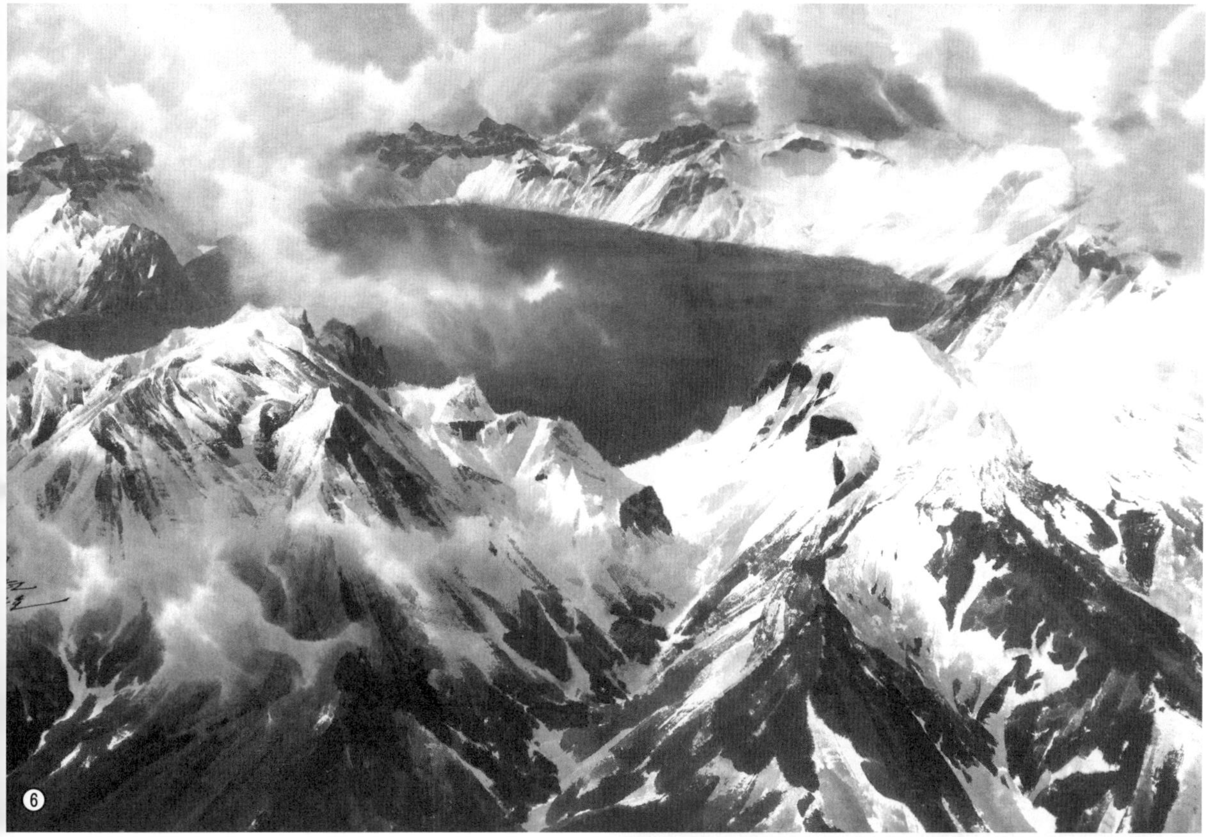

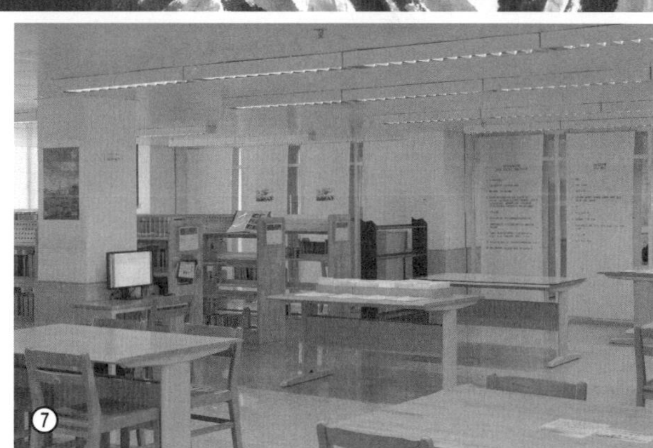

1–4 Hans Haacke, *Die Freiheit wird jetzt einfach gesponsert—aus der Portokasse*
    (Freedom Is Now Simply Going to be Sponsored–Out of Petty Cash), 1990, four photographs.
    Photographs 1 and 2 by Werner Zellien © Hans Haacke/VG Bild-Kunst.
5   Hans Haacke, *Die Freiheit wird jetzt einfach gesponsert—aus der Portokasse*
    (Freedom Is Now Simply Going to be Sponsored–Out of Petty Cash), installation view
    © Hans Haacke/VG Bild-Kunst.
6   Changho Choi, *Mountain Paekdu in Spring*, 2004, printed textile banners.
7   Changho Choi, *Mountain Paekdu in Spring*, installation view.

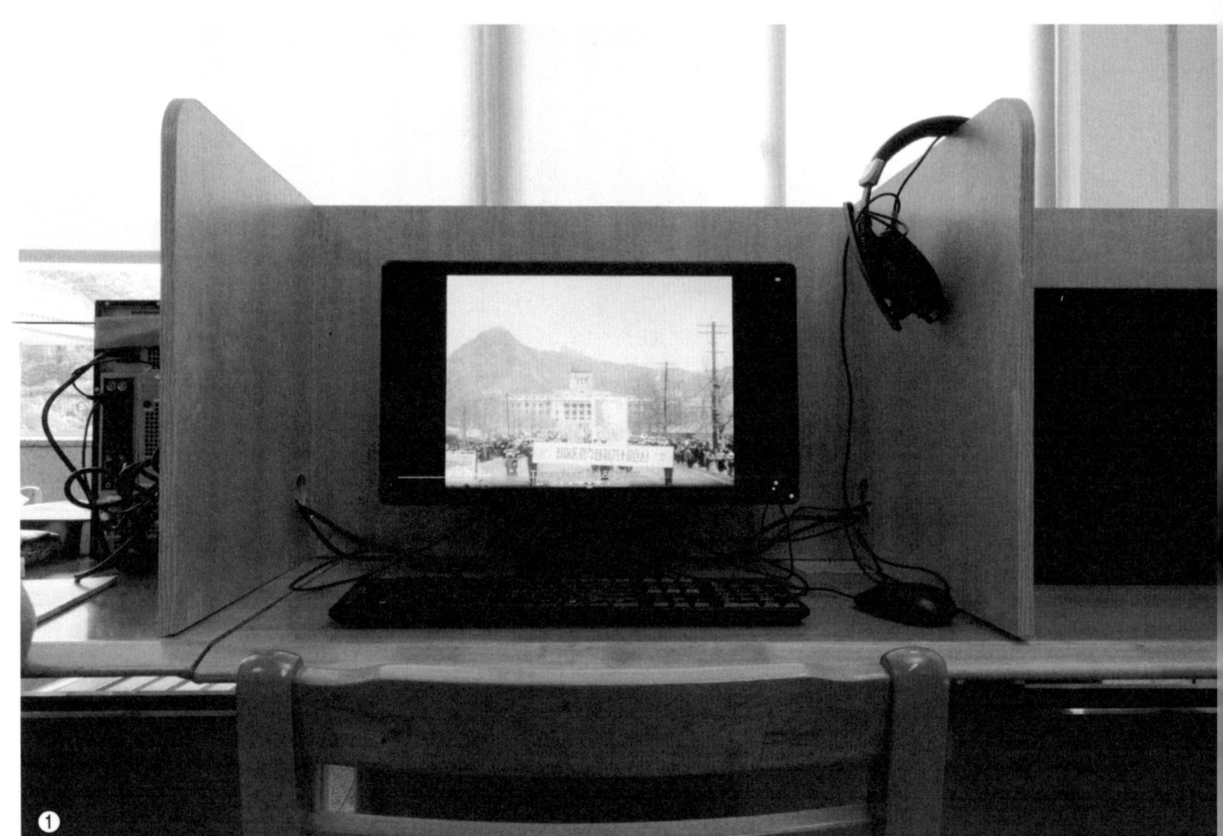

1   Video Program

2   Chankyong Park, *Flying*, 2005, video, 13 min.
3   Kyungman Kim, *Long live his Majesty*, 2002, HD, 13 min.
4   Janet Grau, *Rückblick/Fe-viewing*, 2003, video, 23 min.
5   Gabriele Stötzer, *Künstlerinnengruppe Erfurt, Women Fashion-Object-Show*, 1988,
     from Irmgard Senf, original 8mm film.
6   Liu Ding, *Gift (2)*, 2011, video, 2:51 min.

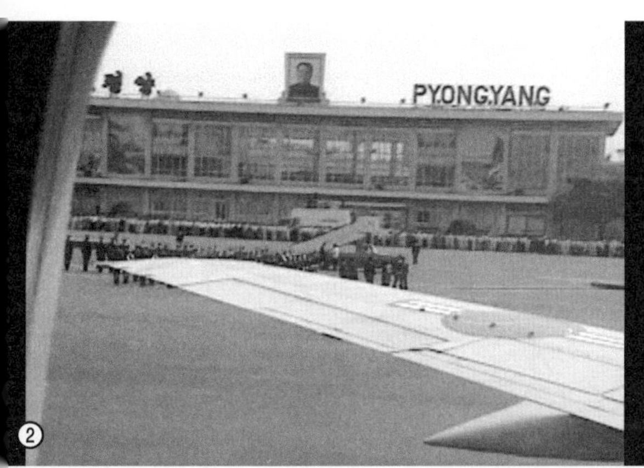

PYONGYANG

②

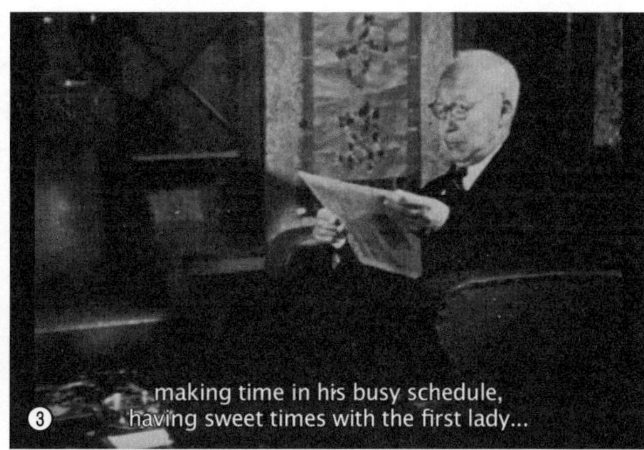

making time in his busy schedule,
having sweet times with the first lady...

③

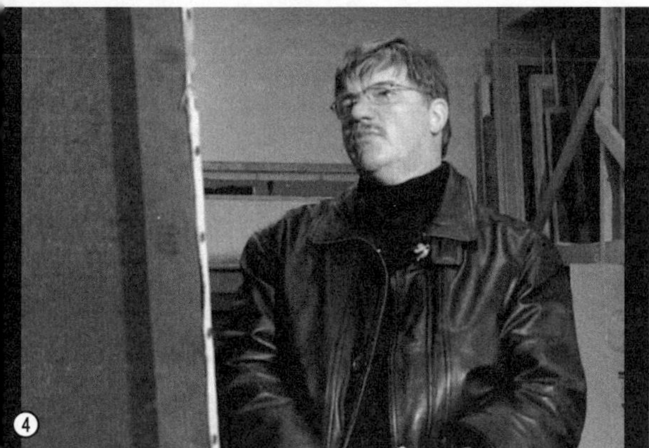

④

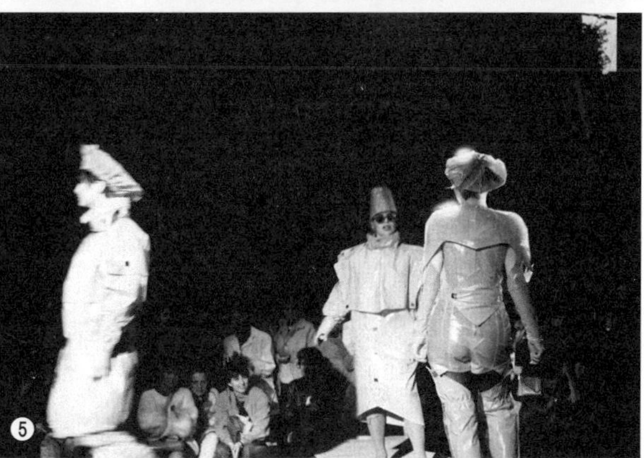

⑤

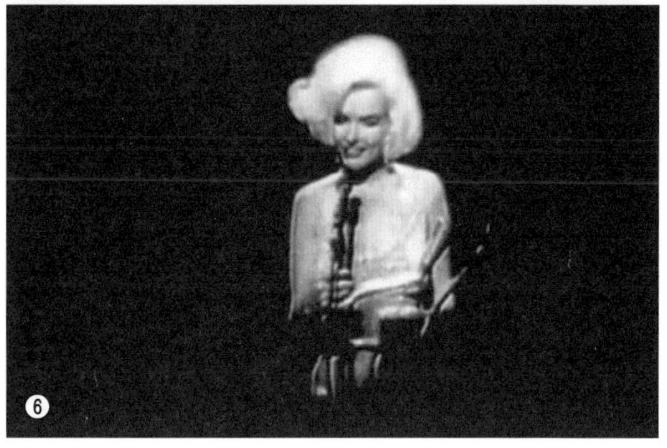

⑥

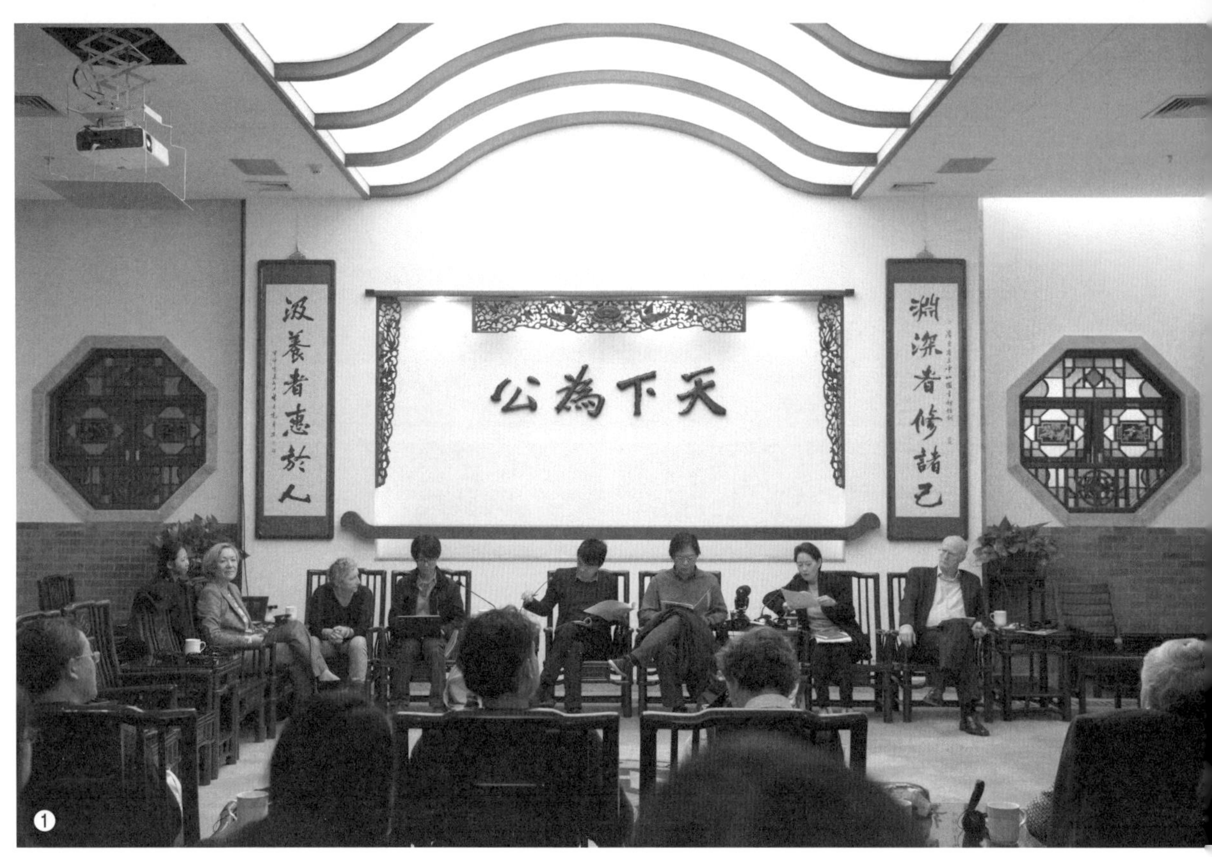

Seminar, December 13, 2015, organized by Sara van der Heide

1   "Open Conversation: on the German Library in Pyongyang; German music and books
     as a means for reunification between North and South Korea,"
     from left to right: Gabriele Gauler, Kyungman Kim, Korean-Chinese interpreter,
     Chankyong Park, Hyunjin Kim, Stefan Dreyer.
2   "Open Conversation": filmmaker Kyungman Kim and interpreter.
3   "Introduction Open Conversation" by Sara van der Heide.
4   "Open Conversation": artist Gabriele Stötzer (left) and Gabriele Gauler, director of
     the Goethe-Institut Hong Kong (right).
5   "Open Conversation": Chankyong Park and Hyunjin Kim.
6   Louwrien Wijers, "Goethe and His Food, the Influence of China on Goethe," 2015, lecture.
7   Egon Hanfstingl, *Blissful Peace Soup*, 2015, cooking performance with local ingredients.
8   Rory Pilgrim, *Complete, Embrace*, 2015, opening and closing ceremony, performed by
     Robyn Haddon, Xiaojuan Xing, and Long Liu.

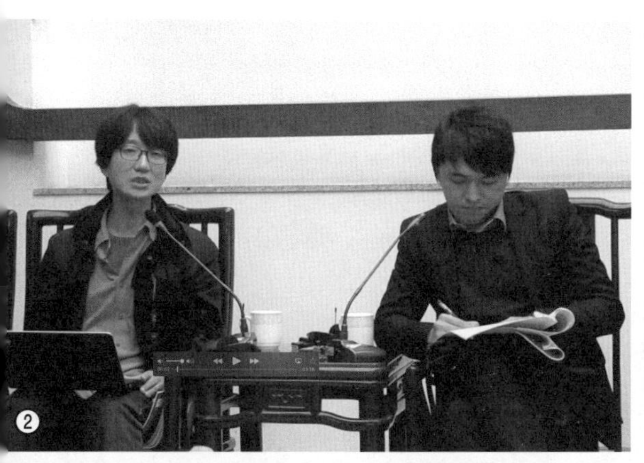

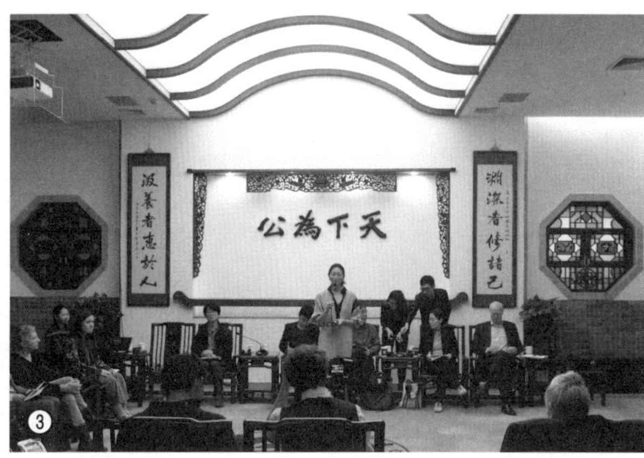

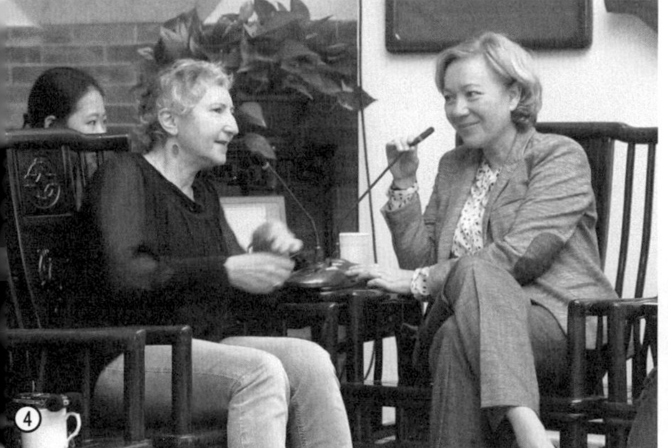

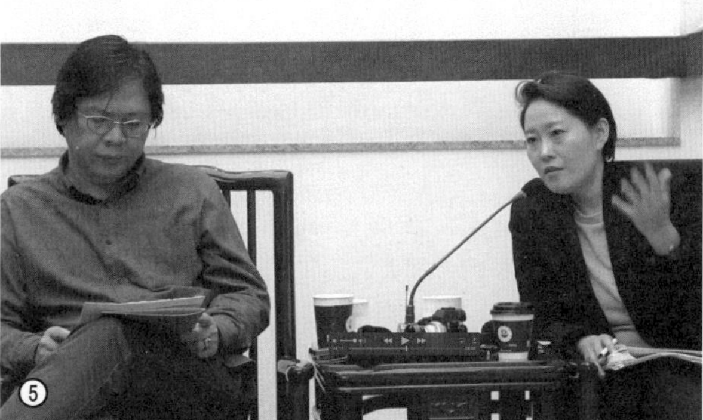

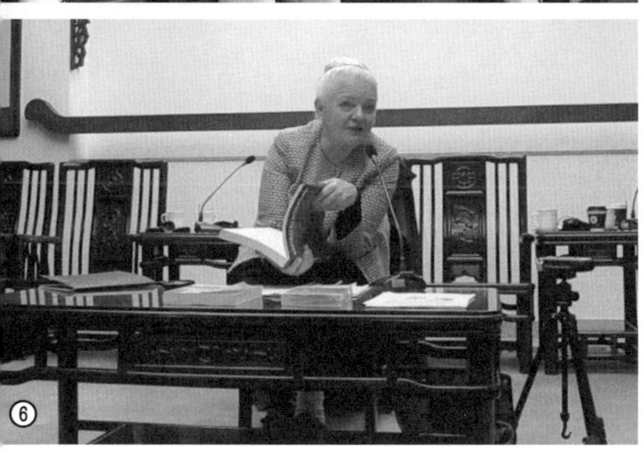

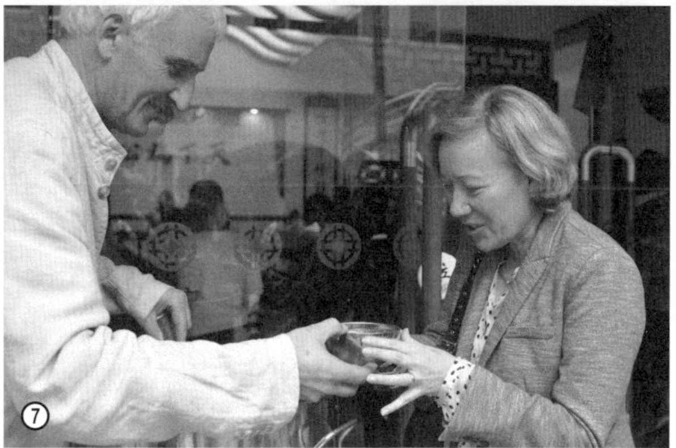

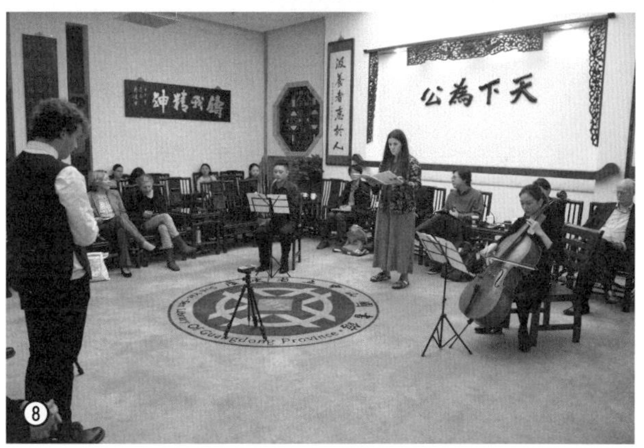

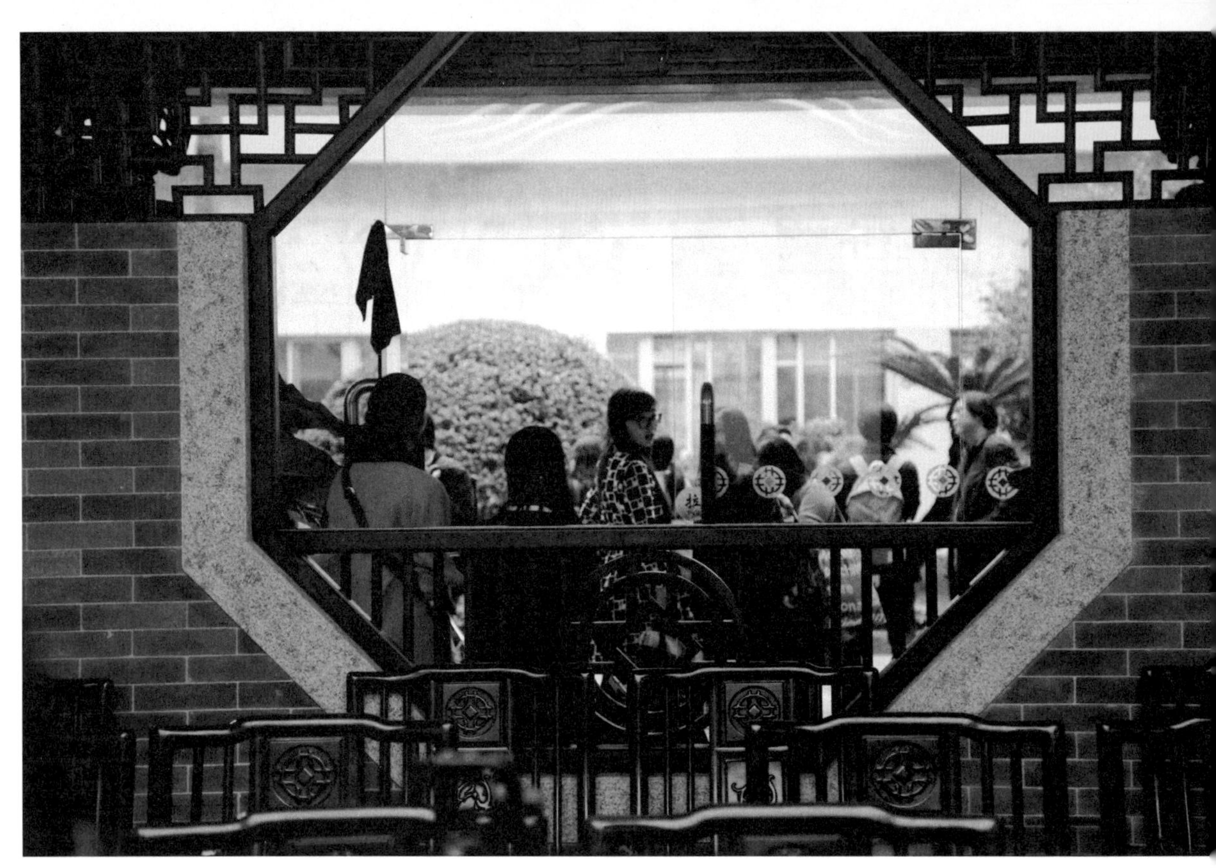